EMMANUEL JOSEPH

Faith-Driven Futures, Integrating Godliness, Morals, and Entrepreneurial Ambitions

Copyright © 2025 by Emmanuel Joseph

All rights reserved. No part of this publication may be reproduced, stored or transmitted in any form or by any means, electronic, mechanical, photocopying, recording, scanning, or otherwise without written permission from the publisher. It is illegal to copy this book, post it to a website, or distribute it by any other means without permission.

First edition

This book was professionally typeset on Reedsy. Find out more at reedsy.com

Contents

1. Chapter 1: The Intersection of Faith and Entrepreneurship — 1
2. Chapter 2: The Ethical Foundation of Faith-Driven Ventures — 3
3. Chapter 3: The Role of Faith in Decision Making — 5
4. Chapter 4: Building a Purpose-Driven Brand — 7
5. Chapter 5: Integrating Faith-Based Leadership Principles — 9
6. Chapter 6: Navigating Challenges and Building Resilience — 11
7. Chapter 7: The Power of Purpose-Driven Innovation — 13
8. Chapter 8: Fostering a Culture of Faith and Excellence — 15
9. Chapter 9: The Role of Faith in Marketing and Branding — 18
10. Chapter 10: The Impact of Faith-Driven Ventures on Society — 20
11. Chapter 11: The Future of Faith-Driven Entrepreneurship — 22
12. Chapter 12: Leaving a Legacy of Faith and Impact — 25

1

Chapter 1: The Intersection of Faith and Entrepreneurship

In a world driven by constant innovation and the relentless pursuit of success, the integration of faith into entrepreneurial endeavors offers a unique perspective that transcends mere profit margins. Faith-driven entrepreneurship is not merely about embedding religious rituals into business practices; it is about grounding one's entrepreneurial journey in a set of unwavering principles that guide every decision and action. This approach demands that entrepreneurs view their ventures as extensions of their moral and spiritual beliefs, ensuring that every step they take aligns with the greater good.

Entrepreneurs who integrate their faith into their business models often find themselves driven by a sense of purpose that goes beyond monetary gain. This purpose fuels their passion, resilience, and commitment to excellence. For instance, a faith-driven entrepreneur may prioritize ethical sourcing of materials, fair labor practices, and environmentally sustainable methods, all of which stem from a belief in stewardship and responsibility towards creation. Such practices not only enhance the credibility of the business but also attract a loyal customer base that values integrity and social responsibility.

The challenges of faith-driven entrepreneurship are multifaceted, as entrepreneurs must navigate the complexities of modern business while remaining true to their moral compass. This often involves making difficult decisions that may not yield immediate financial rewards but contribute to long-term, sustainable growth. It also requires a deep understanding of the market and the ability to innovate within ethical boundaries. The balance between profitability and principles is delicate, but for those who succeed, the rewards are both tangible and intangible.

A key aspect of faith-driven entrepreneurship is the cultivation of a supportive community that shares similar values. This network provides encouragement, resources, and accountability, helping entrepreneurs stay true to their vision. Mentorship from seasoned faith-driven entrepreneurs can be invaluable, offering insights and guidance that are rooted in both business acumen and spiritual wisdom. Such relationships foster a sense of belonging and collective progress towards common goals.

Ultimately, faith-driven entrepreneurship redefines success by integrating godliness, morals, and ambitions into a cohesive framework. It challenges the conventional narratives of entrepreneurship by emphasizing the importance of character, integrity, and purpose. This approach not only transforms businesses but also inspires individuals to lead lives of meaning and impact, leaving a lasting legacy that extends beyond the bottom line.

2

Chapter 2: The Ethical Foundation of Faith-Driven Ventures

Ethics play a pivotal role in faith-driven entrepreneurship, serving as the bedrock upon which all business activities are built. For faith-driven entrepreneurs, ethical considerations are not optional but integral to their operational ethos. This commitment to ethics is reflected in their interactions with employees, customers, suppliers, and the broader community. It ensures that their business practices are transparent, fair, and aligned with their spiritual and moral convictions.

One of the core ethical principles in faith-driven entrepreneurship is honesty. This involves being truthful in advertising, product descriptions, and financial reporting. Honest communication fosters trust and builds a reputation for reliability and integrity. Customers are more likely to remain loyal to businesses that demonstrate honesty, even in challenging situations. For example, admitting a mistake and taking steps to rectify it can enhance a company's credibility and customer satisfaction.

Another fundamental ethical principle is respect. Faith-driven entrepreneurs prioritize respect for all individuals, recognizing their inherent dignity and worth. This respect is evident in fair wages, safe working conditions, and opportunities for professional growth. By creating a positive and inclusive work environment, faith-driven businesses not only attract and retain talented employees but also cultivate a culture of mutual respect and collaboration. Respect extends beyond the workplace to include respectful engagement with customers, suppliers, and the community.

Accountability is also a crucial ethical component in faith-driven entrepreneurship. Entrepreneurs are accountable for their actions and decisions, understanding that they have a responsibility to their stakeholders and the wider society. This accountability is reflected in transparent business practices, ethical sourcing, and sustainable operations. Faith-driven entrepreneurs are mindful of their impact on the environment and strive to minimize their ecological footprint through responsible practices such as waste reduction, energy conservation, and support for sustainable initiatives.

Faith-driven entrepreneurs often find that their ethical commitments lead to innovative solutions and competitive advantages. By prioritizing ethics, they differentiate themselves in the marketplace, attracting customers who value integrity and social responsibility. Ethical practices can also drive innovation, as entrepreneurs seek creative ways to align their business goals with their moral principles. For instance, developing eco-friendly products or implementing fair trade practices can open new markets and enhance brand loyalty.

In conclusion, the ethical foundation of faith-driven ventures is a powerful force that shapes their identity and success. By adhering to principles of honesty, respect, and accountability, faith-driven entrepreneurs create businesses that are not only profitable but also purposeful and impactful. Their commitment to ethics serves as a beacon of hope and inspiration, demonstrating that it is possible to achieve success while staying true to one's values.

3

Chapter 3: The Role of Faith in Decision Making

Decision-making is a critical aspect of entrepreneurship, and for faith-driven entrepreneurs, faith plays a central role in guiding their choices. Faith-driven decision-making involves seeking divine guidance, aligning decisions with moral principles, and considering the broader impact of one's actions. This approach ensures that business decisions are not solely based on profit motives but are also reflective of the entrepreneur's spiritual and ethical convictions.

One of the ways faith influences decision-making is through prayer and reflection. Faith-driven entrepreneurs often turn to prayer as a means of seeking clarity and wisdom when faced with complex decisions. This practice allows them to pause, reflect, and gain a deeper understanding of the situation. It also provides a sense of peace and assurance that they are making decisions in alignment with their faith. For instance, an entrepreneur might pray for guidance when deciding whether to enter a new market or invest in a new product line.

Another aspect of faith-driven decision-making is the consideration of ethical implications. Faith-driven entrepreneurs evaluate the potential impact of their decisions on all stakeholders, including employees, customers, suppliers, and the community. They strive to make choices that promote justice, fairness, and the common good. This ethical discernment involves weighing the potential benefits and harms of each option and choosing the path that aligns with their moral principles. For example, a faith-driven entrepreneur might decide to forego a lucrative business deal that involves unethical practices.

Faith-driven entrepreneurs also recognize the importance of community in decision-making. They seek counsel from trusted advisors, mentors, and peers who share their values and can provide valuable insights. This collaborative approach ensures that decisions are well-informed and consider diverse perspectives. It also fosters a sense of accountability and support, as entrepreneurs are encouraged to remain true to their principles. For instance, a faith-driven entrepreneur might consult with a mentor before making a significant investment decision.

Faith-driven decision-making is characterized by a long-term perspective. Entrepreneurs understand that their choices have lasting consequences and strive to make decisions that contribute to sustainable growth and positive impact. This long-term view encourages them to prioritize values over short-term gains and to invest in practices that build a strong foundation for the future. For example, a faith-driven entrepreneur might invest in employee development programs that enhance skills and foster loyalty.

In summary, the role of faith in decision-making is profound and transformative. Faith-driven entrepreneurs rely on prayer, ethical discernment, community counsel, and a long-term perspective to guide their choices. This approach ensures that their decisions are not only profitable but also aligned with their spiritual and moral values. By integrating faith into their decision-making process, faith-driven entrepreneurs create businesses that are principled, purposeful, and impactful.

4

Chapter 4: Building a Purpose-Driven Brand

In the competitive landscape of modern business, building a purpose-driven brand is a powerful strategy for faith-driven entrepreneurs. A purpose-driven brand goes beyond products and services to communicate the deeper mission and values that the business stands for. This approach resonates with customers who seek meaning and connection in their purchasing decisions and fosters a loyal and engaged customer base.

One of the key elements of building a purpose-driven brand is clearly articulating the brand's mission and values. Faith-driven entrepreneurs must define what their brand stands for and how it aligns with their spiritual and moral beliefs. This clarity of purpose serves as a guiding star for all branding and marketing efforts. For example, a faith-driven business might emphasize its commitment to ethical sourcing, community support, and environmental sustainability in its brand messaging.

Storytelling is a powerful tool for building a purpose-driven brand. Faith-driven entrepreneurs can share their personal journeys, the inspiration behind their ventures, and the impact they seek to make. Authentic and compelling stories create an emotional connection with customers and convey the brand's purpose in a relatable and engaging way. For instance, an entrepreneur might share how their faith motivated them to start a business that empowers marginalized communities through fair trade practices.

Consistency is crucial in building a purpose-driven brand. Faith-driven entrepreneurs must ensure that their actions, policies, and communications align with their stated mission and values. This consistency builds trust and credibility, as customers can see that the brand's purpose is not just a marketing gimmick but a genuine commitment. For example, a faith-driven business that promotes environmental sustainability must demonstrate this commitment through eco-friendly practices, products, and partnerships.

Engagement with the community is another important aspect of building a purpose-driven brand. Faith-driven entrepreneurs can participate in and support initiatives that align with their mission and values. This engagement demonstrates the brand's commitment to making a positive impact and fosters a sense of community and shared purpose. For instance, a faith-driven business might sponsor local events, support charitable organizations, or engage in volunteer activities.

Transparency is also essential in building a purpose-driven brand. Faith-driven entrepreneurs must be open and honest about their practices, challenges, and progress towards their goals. This transparency fosters trust and accountability and allows customers to see the brand's journey and impact. For example, a faith-driven business might publish annual reports on its social and environmental performance, sharing both successes and areas for improvement.

In conclusion, building a purpose-driven brand is a powerful strategy for faith-driven entrepreneurs. By articulating their mission and values, sharing authentic stories, ensuring consistency, engaging with the community, and maintaining transparency, they create brands that resonate with customers and inspire loyalty.

5

Chapter 5: Integrating Faith-Based Leadership Principles

Leadership is a fundamental component of entrepreneurship, and for faith-driven entrepreneurs, leadership is deeply rooted in their spiritual and moral beliefs. Faith-based leadership principles emphasize service, humility, integrity, and compassion, guiding entrepreneurs to lead with purpose and impact. These principles create a leadership style that not only drives business success but also inspires and uplifts others.

One of the key tenets of faith-based leadership is servant leadership. Faith-driven entrepreneurs view their role as leaders as an opportunity to serve others, rather than to wield power. This approach involves prioritizing the needs and well-being of employees, customers, and the community. Servant leaders are attentive, empathetic, and supportive, creating an environment where individuals feel valued and empowered. For example, a faith-driven entrepreneur might implement policies that promote work-life balance, professional development, and employee well-being.

Humility is another essential principle of faith-based leadership. Faith-driven entrepreneurs recognize that their success is not solely a result of their efforts but is also influenced by divine guidance and the contributions of others. This humility fosters a sense of gratitude and openness to learning and growth. Humble leaders are willing to admit their mistakes, seek feedback, and collaborate with others. For instance, a faith-driven entrepreneur might actively engage with employees to understand their perspectives and incorporate their ideas into business strategies.

Integrity is a cornerstone of faith-based leadership. Faith-driven entrepreneurs lead with honesty, transparency, and ethical conduct, ensuring that their actions align with their values. This integrity builds trust and credibility, both within the organization and with external stakeholders. Leaders who demonstrate integrity are consistent in their words and actions, making decisions that reflect their moral principles. For example, a faith-driven entrepreneur might ensure fair pricing, ethical sourcing, and transparent communication with customers.

Compassion is also a vital aspect of faith-based leadership. Faith-driven entrepreneurs lead with empathy and a genuine concern for the well-being of others. This compassion extends to employees, customers, and the broader community, driving leaders to take actions that promote social good and alleviate suffering. Compassionate leaders are approachable, understanding, and supportive, fostering a culture of care and inclusivity. For instance, a faith-driven entrepreneur might support charitable initiatives, volunteer efforts, and community development projects.

In summary, integrating faith-based leadership principles into entrepreneurship creates a leadership style that is purposeful, ethical, and impactful. By embracing servant leadership, humility, integrity, and compassion, faith-driven entrepreneurs lead in a way that inspires and uplifts others. Their leadership not only drives business success but also contributes to the greater good, leaving a positive and lasting legacy.

6

Chapter 6: Navigating Challenges and Building Resilience

Entrepreneurship is inherently challenging, and faith-driven entrepreneurs face unique obstacles as they strive to integrate their spiritual and moral values into their ventures. Navigating these challenges requires resilience, adaptability, and a steadfast commitment to one's faith. By drawing on their spiritual beliefs and practices, faith-driven entrepreneurs can overcome adversity and build businesses that thrive in the face of difficulties.

One of the primary challenges faith-driven entrepreneurs encounter is the pressure to compromise their values for financial gain. In a competitive market, the temptation to cut corners, engage in unethical practices, or prioritize profit over principles can be strong. However, faith-driven entrepreneurs remain resolute in their commitment to integrity, even when it means making difficult decisions that may not yield immediate rewards. This unwavering commitment to values builds a solid foundation for long-term success and trust.

Another challenge is managing the balance between work and spiritual life. Faith-driven entrepreneurs must find ways to integrate their spiritual practices into their busy schedules, ensuring that their faith remains a source of strength and guidance. This balance can be achieved through regular prayer, meditation, and participation in faith-based communities. By prioritizing their spiritual well-being, entrepreneurs can maintain a sense of purpose and perspective, even in the midst of demanding business responsibilities.

Building resilience is crucial for faith-driven entrepreneurs as they navigate the ups and downs of entrepreneurship. Resilience involves the ability to bounce back from setbacks, learn from failures, and remain optimistic in the face of challenges. Faith-driven entrepreneurs draw on their spiritual beliefs to cultivate resilience, finding solace and strength in their faith. For example, an entrepreneur might turn to prayer or scripture for encouragement and guidance during difficult times.

Adaptability is also essential for overcoming challenges. Faith-driven entrepreneurs must be flexible and open to change, willing to pivot their strategies and embrace new opportunities. This adaptability is rooted in a trust in divine guidance and a willingness to let go of rigid plans. Faith-driven entrepreneurs understand that their path may not always unfold as expected, but they remain confident that their faith will lead them in the right direction. For instance, an entrepreneur might explore new markets or innovative products in response to changing customer needs.

Community support is another valuable resource for navigating challenges. Faith-driven entrepreneurs can seek encouragement, advice, and collaboration from their faith-based communities. These communities provide a network of support, offering practical assistance and spiritual encouragement. By engaging with others who share similar values and experiences, entrepreneurs can find strength and motivation to persevere.

In conclusion, navigating challenges and building resilience are essential aspects of faith-driven entrepreneurship. By remaining committed to their values, balancing work and spiritual life, cultivating resilience, embracing adaptability, and seeking community support, faith-driven entrepreneurs can overcome obstacles and build successful, impactful businesses. Their journey serves as a testament to the power of faith in overcoming adversity and achieving lasting success.

7

Chapter 7: The Power of Purpose-Driven Innovation

Innovation is a driving force in entrepreneurship, and for faith-driven entrepreneurs, purpose-driven innovation is a powerful way to create value and make a positive impact. Purpose-driven innovation involves developing new products, services, and solutions that align with the entrepreneur's spiritual and moral values. This approach not only fosters creativity and growth but also contributes to the greater good.

One of the key aspects of purpose-driven innovation is identifying unmet needs and opportunities that align with the entrepreneur's mission and values. Faith-driven entrepreneurs are motivated by a desire to address social, environmental, and ethical challenges through their innovations. For example, an entrepreneur might develop a sustainable product that reduces environmental impact or create a service that supports underserved communities. By focusing on purpose, entrepreneurs can create innovations that resonate with customers and drive positive change.

Collaboration and inclusivity are also important components of purpose-driven innovation. Faith-driven entrepreneurs understand that diverse perspectives and collective efforts can lead to more effective and impactful solutions. They actively seek input from employees, customers, and stakeholders, fostering a culture of collaboration and creativity. For instance, an entrepreneur might involve employees in brainstorming sessions or seek feedback from customers to refine a new product idea.

Purpose-driven innovation is characterized by a commitment to ethical practices. Faith-driven entrepreneurs ensure that their innovations are developed and implemented in a manner that aligns with their values. This involves considering the ethical implications of their innovations, from sourcing materials to manufacturing processes to marketing strategies. For example, an entrepreneur might prioritize fair trade sourcing for a new product or ensure that their marketing practices are honest and transparent.

Continuous improvement is another important aspect of purpose-driven innovation. Faith-driven entrepreneurs are committed to refining and enhancing their products and services to better serve their mission and values. This involves seeking feedback, learning from mistakes, and staying open to new ideas and approaches. By continuously striving for excellence, entrepreneurs can create innovations that are not only effective but also aligned with their purpose.

The impact of purpose-driven innovation extends beyond the business itself to the broader community and society. Faith-driven entrepreneurs recognize that their innovations have the potential to drive positive change and contribute to the greater good. This impact is reflected in improved social and environmental outcomes, enhanced well-being, and increased awareness of ethical and sustainable practices. For instance, an entrepreneur's innovative solution for clean energy might reduce carbon emissions and promote environmental sustainability.

In summary, the power of purpose-driven innovation lies in its ability to create value and drive positive impact. By identifying unmet needs, fostering collaboration, adhering to ethical practices, embracing continuous improvement, and recognizing the broader impact of their innovations, faith-driven entrepreneurs can develop solutions that align with their mission and values. Purpose-driven innovation not only drives business success but also contributes to a better world.

8

Chapter 8: Fostering a Culture of Faith and Excellence

Creating a culture of faith and excellence is essential for faith-driven entrepreneurs who seek to build businesses that reflect their spiritual and moral values. This culture serves as the foundation for all aspects of the business, influencing everything from employee engagement to customer relationships to operational practices. By fostering a culture of faith and excellence, entrepreneurs can create a positive and inspiring work environment that drives success and impact.

One of the key elements of a culture of faith and excellence is a clear and shared vision. Faith-driven entrepreneurs must articulate a vision that aligns with their spiritual and moral values and communicates the purpose and goals of the business. This vision serves as a guiding star for all employees, providing a sense of direction and meaning. For example, an entrepreneur might emphasize the importance of ethical practices, social responsibility, and community support in their vision statement.

Engaging employees in the culture of faith and excellence is crucial for its success. Faith-driven entrepreneurs can create opportunities for employees to connect with the company's mission and values, fostering a sense of ownership and commitment. This engagement can be achieved through regular communication, team-building activities, and professional development programs. For instance, an entrepreneur might organize workshops on ethical leadership or create opportunities for employees to participate in community service projects.

Recognition and reward are also important components of a culture of faith and excellence. Faith-driven entrepreneurs should acknowledge and celebrate the achievements and contributions of their employees, reinforcing the importance of values-driven behavior. This recognition can take various forms, from formal awards and promotions to informal praise and encouragement. By recognizing and rewarding employees who exemplify the company's values, entrepreneurs can reinforce the culture of faith and excellence.

Leading by example is another essential aspect of fostering a culture of faith and excellence. Faith-driven entrepreneurs must demonstrate the values and behaviors they expect from their employees, serving as role models and setting the standard for ethical and purposeful conduct. This leadership by example creates a sense of accountability and inspires by demonstrating commitment to the company's mission and values.

Another key aspect of fostering a culture of faith and excellence is creating an environment that encourages continuous learning and growth. Faith-driven entrepreneurs can provide opportunities for employees to develop their skills, knowledge, and spiritual well-being. This commitment to personal and professional growth fosters a culture of excellence and inspires employees to reach their full potential. For example, an entrepreneur might offer training programs, mentorship opportunities, and spiritual retreats for their team.

Open communication is also essential for fostering a culture of faith and excellence. Faith-driven entrepreneurs must create channels for transparent and honest communication, ensuring that employees feel heard and valued. This open communication fosters trust, collaboration, and a sense of community within the organization. For instance, an entrepreneur might hold regular town hall meetings, encourage feedback, and provide platforms for employees to share their ideas and concerns.

In conclusion, fostering a culture of faith and excellence is a powerful way for faith-driven entrepreneurs to build businesses that reflect their spiritual and moral values. By articulating a clear vision, engaging employees, recognizing and rewarding values-driven behavior, leading by example, promoting continuous learning and growth, and ensuring open communication, entrepreneurs can create a positive and inspiring work environment that drives success and impact.

9

Chapter 9: The Role of Faith in Marketing and Branding

Marketing and branding are crucial components of entrepreneurship, and for faith-driven entrepreneurs, these activities are guided by their spiritual and moral values. Faith-driven marketing and branding involve creating authentic, ethical, and purpose-driven messages that resonate with customers and reflect the entrepreneur's mission and values. This approach builds trust, loyalty, and a strong brand identity.

One of the key principles of faith-driven marketing and branding is authenticity. Faith-driven entrepreneurs must ensure that their marketing messages are genuine and reflective of their true mission and values. This authenticity builds credibility and fosters a deeper connection with customers. For example, an entrepreneur might share stories of how their faith inspires their business practices and the positive impact they seek to make.

Ethical marketing is another important aspect of faith-driven branding. Faith-driven entrepreneurs prioritize honesty, transparency, and fairness in their marketing practices. This involves providing accurate information, avoiding deceptive tactics, and respecting customer privacy. Ethical marketing not only builds trust but also differentiates the brand in a competitive market. For instance, an entrepreneur might ensure that their advertising is

CHAPTER 9: THE ROLE OF FAITH IN MARKETING AND BRANDING

truthful and that their data practices are transparent.

Purpose-driven branding involves creating a brand identity that reflects the entrepreneur's mission and values. Faith-driven entrepreneurs can use their branding to communicate their commitment to social responsibility, environmental sustainability, and ethical practices. This purpose-driven branding resonates with customers who seek meaning and alignment with their own values in their purchasing decisions. For example, an entrepreneur might highlight their commitment to fair trade, eco-friendly products, or community support in their branding.

Engagement with the community is also a key aspect of faith-driven marketing and branding. Faith-driven entrepreneurs can build strong relationships with their customers and the broader community by participating in and supporting initiatives that align with their mission and values. This engagement fosters a sense of community and shared purpose, enhancing brand loyalty and trust. For instance, an entrepreneur might sponsor local events, support charitable organizations, or engage in volunteer activities.

Storytelling is a powerful tool for faith-driven marketing and branding. Faith-driven entrepreneurs can use storytelling to convey their mission, values, and the impact they seek to make. Authentic and compelling stories create an emotional connection with customers and communicate the brand's purpose in a relatable and engaging way. For example, an entrepreneur might share how their faith inspired them to start their business and the positive changes they have achieved.

In summary, faith-driven marketing and branding involve creating authentic, ethical, and purpose-driven messages that reflect the entrepreneur's mission and values. By prioritizing authenticity, ethical marketing, purpose-driven branding, community engagement, and storytelling, faith-driven entrepreneurs can build strong brand identities that resonate with customers and drive loyalty and trust.

10

Chapter 10: The Impact of Faith-Driven Ventures on Society

Faith-driven ventures have the potential to make a significant positive impact on society by addressing social, environmental, and ethical challenges. These ventures are guided by a mission and values that prioritize the common good, inspiring positive change and contributing to a better world. The impact of faith-driven ventures extends beyond their immediate business activities to influence the broader community and society.

One of the key areas of impact for faith-driven ventures is social responsibility. Faith-driven entrepreneurs are committed to addressing social issues and improving the well-being of individuals and communities. This commitment is reflected in their business practices, philanthropic efforts, and community engagement. For example, a faith-driven entrepreneur might support education initiatives, provide job training programs, or invest in affordable housing projects.

Environmental sustainability is another important area of impact for faith-driven ventures. Faith-driven entrepreneurs prioritize environmentally responsible practices, recognizing their responsibility to protect and preserve the natural world. This commitment to sustainability is evident in their sourcing, production, and operational practices. For instance, an entrepreneur

CHAPTER 10: THE IMPACT OF FAITH-DRIVEN VENTURES ON SOCIETY

might use eco-friendly materials, implement energy-efficient processes, and support conservation efforts.

Ethical practices are a cornerstone of faith-driven ventures, influencing their interactions with employees, customers, suppliers, and the broader community. Faith-driven entrepreneurs prioritize fairness, transparency, and respect in all their dealings, building trust and credibility. This ethical conduct fosters positive relationships and contributes to a culture of integrity and accountability. For example, an entrepreneur might ensure fair wages, safe working conditions, and honest communication with customers.

Faith-driven ventures also have a transformative impact on the entrepreneurial landscape, demonstrating that it is possible to achieve success while staying true to one's values. These ventures challenge conventional narratives of entrepreneurship by prioritizing purpose, integrity, and social impact. They serve as role models and inspire other entrepreneurs to adopt similar values-driven approaches. For instance, a successful faith-driven business might mentor and support emerging entrepreneurs who share their mission and values.

The influence of faith-driven ventures extends to their customers, who are inspired and empowered by the brand's mission and values. By choosing to support faith-driven businesses, customers become part of a larger movement for positive change. This consumer support drives demand for ethical and sustainable products and services, encouraging more businesses to adopt values-driven practices. For example, customers who purchase from a faith-driven brand that supports fair trade contribute to the growth of fair trade markets and the well-being of producers.

In conclusion, the impact of faith-driven ventures on society is profound and far-reaching. By addressing social, environmental, and ethical challenges, faith-driven entrepreneurs contribute to a better world and inspire positive change. Their commitment to social responsibility, environmental sustainability, ethical practices, and values-driven entrepreneurship sets a powerful example and encourages others to follow in their footsteps.

11

Chapter 11: The Future of Faith-Driven Entrepreneurship

As the world continues to evolve, the future of faith-driven entrepreneurship holds great promise and potential. Faith-driven entrepreneurs are uniquely positioned to address emerging challenges and opportunities by integrating their spiritual and moral values into their ventures. The future of faith-driven entrepreneurship is characterized by a commitment to innovation, sustainability, and social impact, driving positive change and inspiring others.

One of the key trends shaping the future of faith-driven entrepreneurship is the growing emphasis on sustainability. Faith-driven entrepreneurs recognize the urgent need to address environmental challenges and are at the forefront of developing innovative solutions. This commitment to sustainability is reflected in their products, services, and operational practices. For example, future faith-driven ventures might pioneer new technologies for renewable energy, develop sustainable supply chains, or create zero-waste products.

Social impact will continue to be a central focus of faith-driven entrepreneurship. Faith-driven entrepreneurs are dedicated to making a positive difference in the lives of individuals and communities, addressing social issues such as poverty, education, and healthcare. This focus on social

CHAPTER 11: THE FUTURE OF FAITH-DRIVEN ENTREPRENEURSHIP

impact will drive the development of businesses that prioritize purpose over profit and seek to create lasting change. For instance, future faith-driven ventures might develop social enterprises that provide job opportunities for marginalized populations or create affordable and accessible healthcare solutions.

The integration of technology and faith-driven values will also shape the future of entrepreneurship. Faith-driven entrepreneurs will harness the power of technology to advance their mission and values, leveraging digital tools and platforms to reach wider audiences and drive innovation. This integration will enable faith-driven ventures to scale their impact and create new opportunities for engagement and collaboration. For example, future faith-driven entrepreneurs might use blockchain technology to ensure transparency and traceability in ethical supply chains or develop digital platforms for community support and engagement.

Collaboration and partnerships will play a vital role in the future of faith-driven entrepreneurship. Faith-driven entrepreneurs will seek to build alliances with like-minded organizations, businesses, and communities to amplify their impact and drive collective progress. These collaborations will foster a sense of shared purpose and enable entrepreneurs to leverage diverse resources and expertise. For instance, future faith-driven ventures might form partnerships with nonprofit organizations to address social and environmental challenges or collaborate with other businesses to promote ethical practices and sustainability.

Education and mentorship will be essential for nurturing the next generation of faith-driven entrepreneurs. Established faith-driven entrepreneurs will play a crucial role in providing guidance, support, and inspiration to aspiring entrepreneurs who share their values. This mentorship will help cultivate a new wave of entrepreneurs who are committed to integrating faith, morals, and entrepreneurial ambitions. For example, future faith-driven entrepreneurs might participate in mentorship programs, offer internships, and create educational resources for budding entrepreneurs.

In summary, the future of faith-driven entrepreneurship is bright and promising, characterized by a commitment to sustainability, social impact, technological integration, collaboration, and mentorship. Faith-driven entrepreneurs will continue to lead the way in addressing emerging challenges and opportunities, creating businesses that reflect their spiritual and moral values and inspire positive change.

12

Chapter 12: Leaving a Legacy of Faith and Impact

The ultimate goal of faith-driven entrepreneurship is to leave a lasting legacy of faith, values, and positive impact. Faith-driven entrepreneurs are driven by a sense of purpose and a desire to create a meaningful and enduring difference in the world. This legacy is built through their business practices, relationships, and contributions to society, reflecting their commitment to integrating godliness, morals, and entrepreneurial ambitions.

One of the key aspects of leaving a legacy of faith and impact is creating businesses that stand the test of time and continue to make a positive impact long after the entrepreneur has moved on. Faith-driven entrepreneurs can achieve this by building strong foundations for their businesses, including ethical practices, sustainable operations, and a clear mission and values. By creating businesses that are resilient, adaptable, and purpose-driven, entrepreneurs ensure that their legacy endures.

Investing in people is another crucial aspect of leaving a legacy of faith and impact. Faith-driven entrepreneurs can mentor, support, and inspire the next generation of leaders, passing on their knowledge, experience, and values. This investment in people extends to employees, customers, and the broader community. By fostering a culture of mentorship, education, and empowerment, entrepreneurs can create a ripple effect that spreads their impact far and wide.

Philanthropy and community engagement are also important components of a lasting legacy. Faith-driven entrepreneurs can support charitable initiatives, contribute to community development, and address social and environmental challenges. This philanthropic effort reflects their commitment to making a positive difference and leaves a lasting mark on the world. For example, an entrepreneur might establish a foundation to support education, healthcare, or environmental conservation.

Faith-driven entrepreneurs can also leave a legacy through their advocacy for ethical and values-driven business practices. By championing integrity, social responsibility, and sustainability, entrepreneurs can influence the broader business community and inspire systemic change. This advocacy can take various forms, from public speaking and writing to participation in industry groups and policy discussions. For instance, an entrepreneur might advocate for fair trade practices, environmental regulations, or ethical sourcing standards.

Finally, faith-driven entrepreneurs can leave a legacy of faith and impact by remaining true to their spiritual and moral values throughout their entrepreneurial journey. This unwavering commitment to their faith serves as a powerful example and inspiration to others. By integrating godliness, morals, and entrepreneurial ambitions, faith-driven entrepreneurs demonstrate that it is possible to achieve success while staying true to one's values.

In summary, leaving a legacy of faith and impact is the ultimate goal of faith-driven entrepreneurship. By building resilient and purpose-driven businesses, investing in people, engaging in philanthropy, advocating for ethical practices, and remaining true to their values, faith-driven entrepreneurs create a meaningful and enduring difference in the world. Their legacy reflects their commitment to integrating godliness, morals, and entrepreneurial ambitions, inspiring others to follow in their footsteps and contribute to a better future.

Faith-Driven Futures: Integrating Godliness, Morals, and En-

trepreneurial Ambitions is a compelling exploration of how faith can profoundly shape and drive entrepreneurial endeavors. This book delves into the powerful intersection of spirituality, ethics, and business, offering a unique perspective on how entrepreneurs can build successful ventures rooted in their spiritual and moral values.

Each chapter provides a thorough examination of key concepts, from the ethical foundations of faith-driven ventures to the role of faith in decision-making, leadership, and innovation. The book emphasizes the importance of integrating godliness and morals into all aspects of entrepreneurship, highlighting the transformative impact this approach can have on businesses and society.

Readers will find inspiration and practical guidance on building purpose-driven brands, fostering a culture of faith and excellence, and navigating the challenges of faith-driven entrepreneurship with resilience and adaptability. The book also explores the future of faith-driven entrepreneurship, envisioning a path forward that prioritizes sustainability, social impact, and collaboration.

Ultimately, **Faith-Driven Futures** serves as a beacon for entrepreneurs seeking to harmonize their entrepreneurial ambitions with their spiritual and moral convictions, leaving a lasting legacy of faith and impact. This book is not just a guide but a source of inspiration for those who believe that business can be a force for good when grounded in unwavering principles.

www.ingramcontent.com/pod-product-compliance
Lightning Source LLC
LaVergne TN
LVHW020741090526
838202LV00057BA/6174